THIS BOOK BELONGS TO:

CONTACT INFORMATION	
NAME:	
ADDRESS:	
PHONE:	

START / END DATES

_____ / / _____   TO   _____ / / _____

Dedication

This Christmas Card Address Book is dedicated to all the Christmas Card enthusiasts out there who want to record their Christmas cards sent and received and document their findings in the process.

You are my inspiration for producing books and I'm honored to be a part of keeping all of your Christmas Card notes and records organized.

This journal notebook will help you record the details of sending cards.

Thoughtfully put together with these sections to record: Christmas Gift Checklist and Christmas Cards Sent & Received.

How to Use this Book

The purpose of this book is to keep all of your Christmas Card notes all in one place. It will help keep you organized.

This Christmas Card Address Book will allow you to accurately document every detail about sending your Christmas Cards.

Here are examples of the prompts for you to fill in and write about your experience in this book:

- Christmas Gift Checklist - Checklist for Name, Gift, Sent, Budget, Cost, Total

- Christmas Cards - Checklist for Name, Relation, Address, Bought Card, Sent Card, Received Card

Christmas Gift Checklist

NAME	GIFT	SENT	BUDGET	COST	TOTAL
		○			
		○			
		○			
		○			
		○			
		○			
		○			
		○			
		○			
		○			
		○			
		○			
		○			
		○			
		○			
		○			
		○			
		○			
		○			
		○			
		○			
		○			
		○			
		○			
		○			
		○			
		○			
		○			
		○			
		TOTAL BUDGET		TOTAL COST	

Christmas Gift Checklist

NAME	GIFT	SENT	BUDGET	COST	TOTAL
		○			
		○			
		○			
		○			
		○			
		○			
		○			
		○			
		○			
		○			
		○			
		○			
		○			
		○			
		○			
		○			
		○			
		○			
		○			
		○			
		○			
		○			
		○			
		○			
		○			
		○			
		○			
		TOTAL BUDGET		TOTAL COST	

Christmas Gift Checklist

NAME	GIFT	SENT	BUDGET	COST	TOTAL
		○			
		○			
		○			
		○			
		○			
		○			
		○			
		○			
		○			
		○			
		○			
		○			
		○			
		○			
		○			
		○			
		○			
		○			
		○			
		○			
		○			
		○			
		○			
		○			
		○			
		○			
		○			
		○			
		○			
		TOTAL BUDGET		TOTAL COST	

Christmas Gift Checklist

NAME	GIFT	SENT	BUDGET	COST	TOTAL
		○			
		○			
		○			
		○			
		○			
		○			
		○			
		○			
		○			
		○			
		○			
		○			
		○			
		○			
		○			
		○			
		○			
		○			
		○			
		○			
		○			
		○			
		○			
		○			
		○			
		○			
		○			
		○			
		TOTAL BUDGET		TOTAL COST	

Christmas Gift Checklist

NAME	GIFT	SENT	BUDGET	COST	TOTAL
		○			
		○			
		○			
		○			
		○			
		○			
		○			
		○			
		○			
		○			
		○			
		○			
		○			
		○			
		○			
		○			
		○			
		○			
		○			
		○			
		○			
		○			
		○			
		○			
		○			
		○			
		○			
		○			
		TOTAL BUDGET		TOTAL COST	

Christmas Gift Checklist

NAME	GIFT	SENT	BUDGET	COST	TOTAL
		○			
		○			
		○			
		○			
		○			
		○			
		○			
		○			
		○			
		○			
		○			
		○			
		○			
		○			
		○			
		○			
		○			
		○			
		○			
		○			
		○			
		○			
		○			
		○			
		○			
		TOTAL BUDGET		TOTAL COST	

Christmas Gift Checklist

NAME	GIFT	SENT	BUDGET	COST	TOTAL
		○			
		○			
		○			
		○			
		○			
		○			
		○			
		○			
		○			
		○			
		○			
		○			
		○			
		○			
		○			
		○			
		○			
		○			
		○			
		○			
		○			
		○			
		○			
		○			
		○			
		○			
		○			
		TOTAL BUDGET		TOTAL COST	

Christmas Gift Checklist

NAME	GIFT	SENT	BUDGET	COST	TOTAL
		○			
		○			
		○			
		○			
		○			
		○			
		○			
		○			
		○			
		○			
		○			
		○			
		○			
		○			
		○			
		○			
		○			
		○			
		○			
		○			
		○			
		○			
		○			
		○			
		○			
		○			
		○			
		○			
		TOTAL BUDGET		TOTAL COST	

Christmas Gift Checklist

NAME	GIFT	SENT	BUDGET	COST	TOTAL
		○			
		○			
		○			
		○			
		○			
		○			
		○			
		○			
		○			
		○			
		○			
		○			
		○			
		○			
		○			
		○			
		○			
		○			
		○			
		○			
		○			
		○			
		○			
		○			
		○			
		○			
		○			
		○			
			TOTAL BUDGET		TOTAL COST

Christmas Gift Checklist

NAME	GIFT	SENT	BUDGET	COST	TOTAL
		○			
		○			
		○			
		○			
		○			
		○			
		○			
		○			
		○			
		○			
		○			
		○			
		○			
		○			
		○			
		○			
		○			
		○			
		○			
		○			
		○			
		○			
		○			
		○			
		○			
		○			
		○			
		○			
		TOTAL BUDGET		TOTAL COST	

Christmas Gift Checklist

NAME	GIFT	SENT	BUDGET	COST	TOTAL
		○			
		○			
		○			
		○			
		○			
		○			
		○			
		○			
		○			
		○			
		○			
		○			
		○			
		○			
		○			
		○			
		○			
		○			
		○			
		○			
		○			
		○			
		○			
		○			
		○			
		○			
		○			
		○			
		○			
		TOTAL BUDGET		TOTAL COST	

Christmas Gift Checklist

NAME	GIFT	SENT	BUDGET	COST	TOTAL
		○			
		○			
		○			
		○			
		○			
		○			
		○			
		○			
		○			
		○			
		○			
		○			
		○			
		○			
		○			
		○			
		○			
		○			
		○			
		○			
		○			
		○			
		○			
		○			
		○			
		○			
		○			
		○			
		○			
		TOTAL BUDGET		TOTAL COST	

Christmas Gift Checklist

NAME	GIFT	SENT	BUDGET	COST	TOTAL
		○			
		○			
		○			
		○			
		○			
		○			
		○			
		○			
		○			
		○			
		○			
		○			
		○			
		○			
		○			
		○			
		○			
		○			
		○			
		○			
		○			
		○			
		○			
		○			
		○			
		○			
		○			
		○			
		○			
		TOTAL BUDGET		TOTAL COST	

Christmas Gift Checklist

NAME	GIFT	SENT	BUDGET	COST	TOTAL
		○			
		○			
		○			
		○			
		○			
		○			
		○			
		○			
		○			
		○			
		○			
		○			
		○			
		○			
		○			
		○			
		○			
		○			
		○			
		○			
		○			
		○			
		○			
		○			
		○			
		○			
		○			
		○			
		TOTAL BUDGET		TOTAL COST	

Christmas Gift Checklist

NAME	GIFT	SENT	BUDGET	COST	TOTAL
		○			
		○			
		○			
		○			
		○			
		○			
		○			
		○			
		○			
		○			
		○			
		○			
		○			
		○			
		○			
		○			
		○			
		○			
		○			
		○			
		○			
		○			
		○			
		○			
		○			
		○			
		○			
		○			
		○			
			TOTAL BUDGET		TOTAL COST

Christmas Gift Checklist

NAME	GIFT	SENT	BUDGET	COST	TOTAL
		○			
		○			
		○			
		○			
		○			
		○			
		○			
		○			
		○			
		○			
		○			
		○			
		○			
		○			
		○			
		○			
		○			
		○			
		○			
		○			
		○			
		○			
		○			
		○			
		○			
		○			
		○			
		○			
		○			
			TOTAL BUDGET	TOTAL COST	

Christmas Gift Checklist

NAME	GIFT	SENT	BUDGET	COST	TOTAL
		○			
		○			
		○			
		○			
		○			
		○			
		○			
		○			
		○			
		○			
		○			
		○			
		○			
		○			
		○			
		○			
		○			
		○			
		○			
		○			
		○			
		○			
		○			
		○			
		○			
		○			
		○			
		○			
		○			
			TOTAL BUDGET		TOTAL COST

Christmas Gift Checklist

NAME	GIFT	SENT	BUDGET	COST	TOTAL
		○			
		○			
		○			
		○			
		○			
		○			
		○			
		○			
		○			
		○			
		○			
		○			
		○			
		○			
		○			
		○			
		○			
		○			
		○			
		○			
		○			
		○			
		○			
		○			
		○			
		○			
		○			
		○			
		○			
		TOTAL BUDGET		TOTAL COST	

Christmas Gift Checklist

NAME	GIFT	SENT	BUDGET	COST	TOTAL
		○			
		○			
		○			
		○			
		○			
		○			
		○			
		○			
		○			
		○			
		○			
		○			
		○			
		○			
		○			
		○			
		○			
		○			
		○			
		○			
		○			
		○			
		○			
		○			
		○			
		○			
		○			
			TOTAL BUDGET		TOTAL COST

Christmas Gift Checklist

NAME	GIFT	SENT	BUDGET	COST	TOTAL
		○			
		○			
		○			
		○			
		○			
		○			
		○			
		○			
		○			
		○			
		○			
		○			
		○			
		○			
		○			
		○			
		○			
		○			
		○			
		○			
		○			
		○			
		○			
		○			
		○			
		○			
		TOTAL BUDGET		TOTAL COST	

Christmas Cards

NAME					
RELATION					
ADDRESS			ZIP CODE		
BOUGHT CARD	○	SENT THE CARD	○	RECEIVED CARD	○

NAME					
RELATION					
ADDRESS			ZIP CODE		
BOUGHT CARD	○	SENT THE CARD	○	RECEIVED CARD	○

NAME					
RELATION					
ADDRESS			ZIP CODE		
BOUGHT CARD	○	SENT THE CARD	○	RECEIVED CARD	○

NAME					
RELATION					
ADDRESS			ZIP CODE		
BOUGHT CARD	○	SENT THE CARD	○	RECEIVED CARD	○

NAME					
RELATION					
ADDRESS			ZIP CODE		
BOUGHT CARD	○	SENT THE CARD	○	RECEIVED CARD	○

NAME					
RELATION					
ADDRESS			ZIP CODE		
BOUGHT CARD	○	SENT THE CARD	○	RECEIVED CARD	○

NAME					
RELATION					
ADDRESS			ZIP CODE		
BOUGHT CARD	○	SENT THE CARD	○	RECEIVED CARD	○

Christmas Cards

NAME	
RELATION	
ADDRESS	ZIP CODE
BOUGHT CARD ○	SENT THE CARD ○	RECEIVED CARD ○

NAME	
RELATION	
ADDRESS	ZIP CODE
BOUGHT CARD ○	SENT THE CARD ○	RECEIVED CARD ○

NAME	
RELATION	
ADDRESS	ZIP CODE
BOUGHT CARD ○	SENT THE CARD ○	RECEIVED CARD ○

NAME	
RELATION	
ADDRESS	ZIP CODE
BOUGHT CARD ○	SENT THE CARD ○	RECEIVED CARD ○

NAME	
RELATION	
ADDRESS	ZIP CODE
BOUGHT CARD ○	SENT THE CARD ○	RECEIVED CARD ○

NAME	
RELATION	
ADDRESS	ZIP CODE
BOUGHT CARD ○	SENT THE CARD ○	RECEIVED CARD ○

NAME	
RELATION	
ADDRESS	ZIP CODE
BOUGHT CARD ○	SENT THE CARD ○	RECEIVED CARD ○

Christmas Cards

NAME				
RELATION				
ADDRESS			ZIP CODE	
BOUGHT CARD	○	SENT THE CARD	○	RECEIVED CARD	○

NAME				
RELATION				
ADDRESS			ZIP CODE	
BOUGHT CARD	○	SENT THE CARD	○	RECEIVED CARD	○

NAME				
RELATION				
ADDRESS			ZIP CODE	
BOUGHT CARD	○	SENT THE CARD	○	RECEIVED CARD	○

NAME				
RELATION				
ADDRESS			ZIP CODE	
BOUGHT CARD	○	SENT THE CARD	○	RECEIVED CARD	○

NAME				
RELATION				
ADDRESS			ZIP CODE	
BOUGHT CARD	○	SENT THE CARD	○	RECEIVED CARD	○

NAME				
RELATION				
ADDRESS			ZIP CODE	
BOUGHT CARD	○	SENT THE CARD	○	RECEIVED CARD	○

NAME				
RELATION				
ADDRESS			ZIP CODE	
BOUGHT CARD	○	SENT THE CARD	○	RECEIVED CARD	○

Christmas Cards

NAME						
RELATION						
ADDRESS				ZIP CODE		
BOUGHT CARD	○	SENT THE CARD	○	RECEIVED CARD	○	

NAME						
RELATION						
ADDRESS				ZIP CODE		
BOUGHT CARD	○	SENT THE CARD	○	RECEIVED CARD	○	

NAME						
RELATION						
ADDRESS				ZIP CODE		
BOUGHT CARD	○	SENT THE CARD	○	RECEIVED CARD	○	

NAME						
RELATION						
ADDRESS				ZIP CODE		
BOUGHT CARD	○	SENT THE CARD	○	RECEIVED CARD	○	

NAME						
RELATION						
ADDRESS				ZIP CODE		
BOUGHT CARD	○	SENT THE CARD	○	RECEIVED CARD	○	

NAME						
RELATION						
ADDRESS				ZIP CODE		
BOUGHT CARD	○	SENT THE CARD	○	RECEIVED CARD	○	

NAME						
RELATION						
ADDRESS				ZIP CODE		
BOUGHT CARD	○	SENT THE CARD	○	RECEIVED CARD	○	

Christmas Cards

NAME						
RELATION						
ADDRESS				ZIP CODE		
BOUGHT CARD	○	SENT THE CARD	○	RECEIVED CARD		○

NAME						
RELATION						
ADDRESS				ZIP CODE		
BOUGHT CARD	○	SENT THE CARD	○	RECEIVED CARD		○

NAME						
RELATION						
ADDRESS				ZIP CODE		
BOUGHT CARD	○	SENT THE CARD	○	RECEIVED CARD		○

NAME						
RELATION						
ADDRESS				ZIP CODE		
BOUGHT CARD	○	SENT THE CARD	○	RECEIVED CARD		○

NAME						
RELATION						
ADDRESS				ZIP CODE		
BOUGHT CARD	○	SENT THE CARD	○	RECEIVED CARD		○

NAME						
RELATION						
ADDRESS				ZIP CODE		
BOUGHT CARD	○	SENT THE CARD	○	RECEIVED CARD		○

NAME						
RELATION						
ADDRESS				ZIP CODE		
BOUGHT CARD	○	SENT THE CARD	○	RECEIVED CARD		○

Christmas Cards

NAME					
RELATION					
ADDRESS			ZIP CODE		
BOUGHT CARD	○	SENT THE CARD	○	RECEIVED CARD	○

NAME					
RELATION					
ADDRESS			ZIP CODE		
BOUGHT CARD	○	SENT THE CARD	○	RECEIVED CARD	○

NAME					
RELATION					
ADDRESS			ZIP CODE		
BOUGHT CARD	○	SENT THE CARD	○	RECEIVED CARD	○

NAME					
RELATION					
ADDRESS			ZIP CODE		
BOUGHT CARD	○	SENT THE CARD	○	RECEIVED CARD	○

NAME					
RELATION					
ADDRESS			ZIP CODE		
BOUGHT CARD	○	SENT THE CARD	○	RECEIVED CARD	○

NAME					
RELATION					
ADDRESS			ZIP CODE		
BOUGHT CARD	○	SENT THE CARD	○	RECEIVED CARD	○

NAME					
RELATION					
ADDRESS			ZIP CODE		
BOUGHT CARD	○	SENT THE CARD	○	RECEIVED CARD	○

Christmas Cards

NAME					
RELATION					
ADDRESS				ZIP CODE	
BOUGHT CARD	○	SENT THE CARD	○	RECEIVED CARD	○

NAME					
RELATION					
ADDRESS				ZIP CODE	
BOUGHT CARD	○	SENT THE CARD	○	RECEIVED CARD	○

NAME					
RELATION					
ADDRESS				ZIP CODE	
BOUGHT CARD	○	SENT THE CARD	○	RECEIVED CARD	○

NAME					
RELATION					
ADDRESS				ZIP CODE	
BOUGHT CARD	○	SENT THE CARD	○	RECEIVED CARD	○

NAME					
RELATION					
ADDRESS				ZIP CODE	
BOUGHT CARD	○	SENT THE CARD	○	RECEIVED CARD	○

NAME					
RELATION					
ADDRESS				ZIP CODE	
BOUGHT CARD	○	SENT THE CARD	○	RECEIVED CARD	○

NAME					
RELATION					
ADDRESS				ZIP CODE	
BOUGHT CARD	○	SENT THE CARD	○	RECEIVED CARD	○

Christmas Cards

NAME					
RELATION					
ADDRESS			ZIP CODE		
BOUGHT CARD	○	SENT THE CARD	○	RECEIVED CARD	○

NAME					
RELATION					
ADDRESS			ZIP CODE		
BOUGHT CARD	○	SENT THE CARD	○	RECEIVED CARD	○

NAME					
RELATION					
ADDRESS			ZIP CODE		
BOUGHT CARD	○	SENT THE CARD	○	RECEIVED CARD	○

NAME					
RELATION					
ADDRESS			ZIP CODE		
BOUGHT CARD	○	SENT THE CARD	○	RECEIVED CARD	○

NAME					
RELATION					
ADDRESS			ZIP CODE		
BOUGHT CARD	○	SENT THE CARD	○	RECEIVED CARD	○

NAME					
RELATION					
ADDRESS			ZIP CODE		
BOUGHT CARD	○	SENT THE CARD	○	RECEIVED CARD	○

NAME					
RELATION					
ADDRESS			ZIP CODE		
BOUGHT CARD	○	SENT THE CARD	○	RECEIVED CARD	○

Christmas Cards

NAME					
RELATION					
ADDRESS			ZIP CODE		
BOUGHT CARD	○	SENT THE CARD	○	RECEIVED CARD	○

NAME					
RELATION					
ADDRESS			ZIP CODE		
BOUGHT CARD	○	SENT THE CARD	○	RECEIVED CARD	○

NAME					
RELATION					
ADDRESS			ZIP CODE		
BOUGHT CARD	○	SENT THE CARD	○	RECEIVED CARD	○

NAME					
RELATION					
ADDRESS			ZIP CODE		
BOUGHT CARD	○	SENT THE CARD	○	RECEIVED CARD	○

NAME					
RELATION					
ADDRESS			ZIP CODE		
BOUGHT CARD	○	SENT THE CARD	○	RECEIVED CARD	○

NAME					
RELATION					
ADDRESS			ZIP CODE		
BOUGHT CARD	○	SENT THE CARD	○	RECEIVED CARD	○

NAME					
RELATION					
ADDRESS			ZIP CODE		
BOUGHT CARD	○	SENT THE CARD	○	RECEIVED CARD	○

Christmas Cards

NAME						
RELATION						
ADDRESS				ZIP CODE		
BOUGHT CARD	○	SENT THE CARD	○	RECEIVED CARD		○

NAME						
RELATION						
ADDRESS				ZIP CODE		
BOUGHT CARD	○	SENT THE CARD	○	RECEIVED CARD		○

NAME						
RELATION						
ADDRESS				ZIP CODE		
BOUGHT CARD	○	SENT THE CARD	○	RECEIVED CARD		○

NAME						
RELATION						
ADDRESS				ZIP CODE		
BOUGHT CARD	○	SENT THE CARD	○	RECEIVED CARD		○

NAME						
RELATION						
ADDRESS				ZIP CODE		
BOUGHT CARD	○	SENT THE CARD	○	RECEIVED CARD		○

NAME						
RELATION						
ADDRESS				ZIP CODE		
BOUGHT CARD	○	SENT THE CARD	○	RECEIVED CARD		○

NAME						
RELATION						
ADDRESS				ZIP CODE		
BOUGHT CARD	○	SENT THE CARD	○	RECEIVED CARD		○

Christmas Cards

NAME					
RELATION					
ADDRESS			ZIP CODE		
BOUGHT CARD	○	SENT THE CARD	○	RECEIVED CARD	○

NAME					
RELATION					
ADDRESS			ZIP CODE		
BOUGHT CARD	○	SENT THE CARD	○	RECEIVED CARD	○

NAME					
RELATION					
ADDRESS			ZIP CODE		
BOUGHT CARD	○	SENT THE CARD	○	RECEIVED CARD	○

NAME					
RELATION					
ADDRESS			ZIP CODE		
BOUGHT CARD	○	SENT THE CARD	○	RECEIVED CARD	○

NAME					
RELATION					
ADDRESS			ZIP CODE		
BOUGHT CARD	○	SENT THE CARD	○	RECEIVED CARD	○

NAME					
RELATION					
ADDRESS			ZIP CODE		
BOUGHT CARD	○	SENT THE CARD	○	RECEIVED CARD	○

NAME					
RELATION					
ADDRESS			ZIP CODE		
BOUGHT CARD	○	SENT THE CARD	○	RECEIVED CARD	○

Christmas Cards

NAME					
RELATION					
ADDRESS				ZIP CODE	
BOUGHT CARD	○	SENT THE CARD	○	RECEIVED CARD	○

NAME					
RELATION					
ADDRESS				ZIP CODE	
BOUGHT CARD	○	SENT THE CARD	○	RECEIVED CARD	○

NAME					
RELATION					
ADDRESS				ZIP CODE	
BOUGHT CARD	○	SENT THE CARD	○	RECEIVED CARD	○

NAME					
RELATION					
ADDRESS				ZIP CODE	
BOUGHT CARD	○	SENT THE CARD	○	RECEIVED CARD	○

NAME					
RELATION					
ADDRESS				ZIP CODE	
BOUGHT CARD	○	SENT THE CARD	○	RECEIVED CARD	○

NAME					
RELATION					
ADDRESS				ZIP CODE	
BOUGHT CARD	○	SENT THE CARD	○	RECEIVED CARD	○

NAME					
RELATION					
ADDRESS				ZIP CODE	
BOUGHT CARD	○	SENT THE CARD	○	RECEIVED CARD	○

Christmas Cards

NAME					
RELATION					
ADDRESS			ZIP CODE		
BOUGHT CARD	○	SENT THE CARD	○	RECEIVED CARD	○

NAME					
RELATION					
ADDRESS			ZIP CODE		
BOUGHT CARD	○	SENT THE CARD	○	RECEIVED CARD	○

NAME					
RELATION					
ADDRESS			ZIP CODE		
BOUGHT CARD	○	SENT THE CARD	○	RECEIVED CARD	○

NAME					
RELATION					
ADDRESS			ZIP CODE		
BOUGHT CARD	○	SENT THE CARD	○	RECEIVED CARD	○

NAME					
RELATION					
ADDRESS			ZIP CODE		
BOUGHT CARD	○	SENT THE CARD	○	RECEIVED CARD	○

NAME					
RELATION					
ADDRESS			ZIP CODE		
BOUGHT CARD	○	SENT THE CARD	○	RECEIVED CARD	○

NAME					
RELATION					
ADDRESS			ZIP CODE		
BOUGHT CARD	○	SENT THE CARD	○	RECEIVED CARD	○

Christmas Cards

NAME						
RELATION						
ADDRESS				ZIP CODE		
BOUGHT CARD	○	SENT THE CARD	○	RECEIVED CARD		○

NAME						
RELATION						
ADDRESS				ZIP CODE		
BOUGHT CARD	○	SENT THE CARD	○	RECEIVED CARD		○

NAME						
RELATION						
ADDRESS				ZIP CODE		
BOUGHT CARD	○	SENT THE CARD	○	RECEIVED CARD		○

NAME						
RELATION						
ADDRESS				ZIP CODE		
BOUGHT CARD	○	SENT THE CARD	○	RECEIVED CARD		○

NAME						
RELATION						
ADDRESS				ZIP CODE		
BOUGHT CARD	○	SENT THE CARD	○	RECEIVED CARD		○

NAME						
RELATION						
ADDRESS				ZIP CODE		
BOUGHT CARD	○	SENT THE CARD	○	RECEIVED CARD		○

NAME						
RELATION						
ADDRESS				ZIP CODE		
BOUGHT CARD	○	SENT THE CARD	○	RECEIVED CARD		○

Christmas Cards

NAME					
RELATION					
ADDRESS			ZIP CODE		
BOUGHT CARD	○	SENT THE CARD	○	RECEIVED CARD	○

NAME					
RELATION					
ADDRESS			ZIP CODE		
BOUGHT CARD	○	SENT THE CARD	○	RECEIVED CARD	○

NAME					
RELATION					
ADDRESS			ZIP CODE		
BOUGHT CARD	○	SENT THE CARD	○	RECEIVED CARD	○

NAME					
RELATION					
ADDRESS			ZIP CODE		
BOUGHT CARD	○	SENT THE CARD	○	RECEIVED CARD	○

NAME					
RELATION					
ADDRESS			ZIP CODE		
BOUGHT CARD	○	SENT THE CARD	○	RECEIVED CARD	○

NAME					
RELATION					
ADDRESS			ZIP CODE		
BOUGHT CARD	○	SENT THE CARD	○	RECEIVED CARD	○

NAME					
RELATION					
ADDRESS			ZIP CODE		
BOUGHT CARD	○	SENT THE CARD	○	RECEIVED CARD	○

Christmas Cards

NAME					
RELATION					
ADDRESS			ZIP CODE		
BOUGHT CARD	○	SENT THE CARD	○	RECEIVED CARD	○

NAME					
RELATION					
ADDRESS			ZIP CODE		
BOUGHT CARD	○	SENT THE CARD	○	RECEIVED CARD	○

NAME					
RELATION					
ADDRESS			ZIP CODE		
BOUGHT CARD	○	SENT THE CARD	○	RECEIVED CARD	○

NAME					
RELATION					
ADDRESS			ZIP CODE		
BOUGHT CARD	○	SENT THE CARD	○	RECEIVED CARD	○

NAME					
RELATION					
ADDRESS			ZIP CODE		
BOUGHT CARD	○	SENT THE CARD	○	RECEIVED CARD	○

NAME					
RELATION					
ADDRESS			ZIP CODE		
BOUGHT CARD	○	SENT THE CARD	○	RECEIVED CARD	○

NAME					
RELATION					
ADDRESS			ZIP CODE		
BOUGHT CARD	○	SENT THE CARD	○	RECEIVED CARD	○

Christmas Cards

NAME						
RELATION						
ADDRESS				ZIP CODE		
BOUGHT CARD	○	SENT THE CARD	○	RECEIVED CARD		○

NAME						
RELATION						
ADDRESS				ZIP CODE		
BOUGHT CARD	○	SENT THE CARD	○	RECEIVED CARD		○

NAME						
RELATION						
ADDRESS				ZIP CODE		
BOUGHT CARD	○	SENT THE CARD	○	RECEIVED CARD		○

NAME						
RELATION						
ADDRESS				ZIP CODE		
BOUGHT CARD	○	SENT THE CARD	○	RECEIVED CARD		○

NAME						
RELATION						
ADDRESS				ZIP CODE		
BOUGHT CARD	○	SENT THE CARD	○	RECEIVED CARD		○

NAME						
RELATION						
ADDRESS				ZIP CODE		
BOUGHT CARD	○	SENT THE CARD	○	RECEIVED CARD		○

NAME						
RELATION						
ADDRESS				ZIP CODE		
BOUGHT CARD	○	SENT THE CARD	○	RECEIVED CARD		○

Christmas Cards

NAME							
RELATION							
ADDRESS					ZIP CODE		
BOUGHT CARD		○	SENT THE CARD	○	RECEIVED CARD		○

NAME							
RELATION							
ADDRESS					ZIP CODE		
BOUGHT CARD		○	SENT THE CARD	○	RECEIVED CARD		○

NAME							
RELATION							
ADDRESS					ZIP CODE		
BOUGHT CARD		○	SENT THE CARD	○	RECEIVED CARD		○

NAME							
RELATION							
ADDRESS					ZIP CODE		
BOUGHT CARD		○	SENT THE CARD	○	RECEIVED CARD		○

NAME							
RELATION							
ADDRESS					ZIP CODE		
BOUGHT CARD		○	SENT THE CARD	○	RECEIVED CARD		○

NAME							
RELATION							
ADDRESS					ZIP CODE		
BOUGHT CARD		○	SENT THE CARD	○	RECEIVED CARD		○

NAME							
RELATION							
ADDRESS					ZIP CODE		
BOUGHT CARD		○	SENT THE CARD	○	RECEIVED CARD		○

Christmas Cards

NAME					
RELATION					
ADDRESS			ZIP CODE		
BOUGHT CARD	○	SENT THE CARD	○	RECEIVED CARD	○

NAME					
RELATION					
ADDRESS			ZIP CODE		
BOUGHT CARD	○	SENT THE CARD	○	RECEIVED CARD	○

NAME					
RELATION					
ADDRESS			ZIP CODE		
BOUGHT CARD	○	SENT THE CARD	○	RECEIVED CARD	○

NAME					
RELATION					
ADDRESS			ZIP CODE		
BOUGHT CARD	○	SENT THE CARD	○	RECEIVED CARD	○

NAME					
RELATION					
ADDRESS			ZIP CODE		
BOUGHT CARD	○	SENT THE CARD	○	RECEIVED CARD	○

NAME					
RELATION					
ADDRESS			ZIP CODE		
BOUGHT CARD	○	SENT THE CARD	○	RECEIVED CARD	○

NAME					
RELATION					
ADDRESS			ZIP CODE		
BOUGHT CARD	○	SENT THE CARD	○	RECEIVED CARD	○

Christmas Cards

NAME						
RELATION						
ADDRESS				ZIP CODE		
BOUGHT CARD	○	SENT THE CARD	○	RECEIVED CARD		○

NAME						
RELATION						
ADDRESS				ZIP CODE		
BOUGHT CARD	○	SENT THE CARD	○	RECEIVED CARD		○

NAME						
RELATION						
ADDRESS				ZIP CODE		
BOUGHT CARD	○	SENT THE CARD	○	RECEIVED CARD		○

NAME						
RELATION						
ADDRESS				ZIP CODE		
BOUGHT CARD	○	SENT THE CARD	○	RECEIVED CARD		○

NAME						
RELATION						
ADDRESS				ZIP CODE		
BOUGHT CARD	○	SENT THE CARD	○	RECEIVED CARD		○

NAME						
RELATION						
ADDRESS				ZIP CODE		
BOUGHT CARD	○	SENT THE CARD	○	RECEIVED CARD		○

NAME						
RELATION						
ADDRESS				ZIP CODE		
BOUGHT CARD	○	SENT THE CARD	○	RECEIVED CARD		○

Christmas Cards

NAME				
RELATION				
ADDRESS			ZIP CODE	
BOUGHT CARD	○	SENT THE CARD	○	RECEIVED CARD	○

NAME				
RELATION				
ADDRESS			ZIP CODE	
BOUGHT CARD	○	SENT THE CARD	○	RECEIVED CARD	○

NAME				
RELATION				
ADDRESS			ZIP CODE	
BOUGHT CARD	○	SENT THE CARD	○	RECEIVED CARD	○

NAME				
RELATION				
ADDRESS			ZIP CODE	
BOUGHT CARD	○	SENT THE CARD	○	RECEIVED CARD	○

NAME				
RELATION				
ADDRESS			ZIP CODE	
BOUGHT CARD	○	SENT THE CARD	○	RECEIVED CARD	○

NAME				
RELATION				
ADDRESS			ZIP CODE	
BOUGHT CARD	○	SENT THE CARD	○	RECEIVED CARD	○

NAME				
RELATION				
ADDRESS			ZIP CODE	
BOUGHT CARD	○	SENT THE CARD	○	RECEIVED CARD	○

Christmas Cards

NAME						
RELATION						
ADDRESS				ZIP CODE		
BOUGHT CARD	○	SENT THE CARD	○	RECEIVED CARD		○

NAME						
RELATION						
ADDRESS				ZIP CODE		
BOUGHT CARD	○	SENT THE CARD	○	RECEIVED CARD		○

NAME						
RELATION						
ADDRESS				ZIP CODE		
BOUGHT CARD	○	SENT THE CARD	○	RECEIVED CARD		○

NAME						
RELATION						
ADDRESS				ZIP CODE		
BOUGHT CARD	○	SENT THE CARD	○	RECEIVED CARD		○

NAME						
RELATION						
ADDRESS				ZIP CODE		
BOUGHT CARD	○	SENT THE CARD	○	RECEIVED CARD		○

NAME						
RELATION						
ADDRESS				ZIP CODE		
BOUGHT CARD	○	SENT THE CARD	○	RECEIVED CARD		○

NAME						
RELATION						
ADDRESS				ZIP CODE		
BOUGHT CARD	○	SENT THE CARD	○	RECEIVED CARD		○

Christmas Cards

NAME					
RELATION					
ADDRESS			ZIP CODE		
BOUGHT CARD	○	SENT THE CARD	○	RECEIVED CARD	○

NAME					
RELATION					
ADDRESS			ZIP CODE		
BOUGHT CARD	○	SENT THE CARD	○	RECEIVED CARD	○

NAME					
RELATION					
ADDRESS			ZIP CODE		
BOUGHT CARD	○	SENT THE CARD	○	RECEIVED CARD	○

NAME					
RELATION					
ADDRESS			ZIP CODE		
BOUGHT CARD	○	SENT THE CARD	○	RECEIVED CARD	○

NAME					
RELATION					
ADDRESS			ZIP CODE		
BOUGHT CARD	○	SENT THE CARD	○	RECEIVED CARD	○

NAME					
RELATION					
ADDRESS			ZIP CODE		
BOUGHT CARD	○	SENT THE CARD	○	RECEIVED CARD	○

NAME					
RELATION					
ADDRESS			ZIP CODE		
BOUGHT CARD	○	SENT THE CARD	○	RECEIVED CARD	○

Christmas Cards

NAME							
RELATION							
ADDRESS					ZIP CODE		
BOUGHT CARD		○	SENT THE CARD	○	RECEIVED CARD		○

NAME							
RELATION							
ADDRESS					ZIP CODE		
BOUGHT CARD		○	SENT THE CARD	○	RECEIVED CARD		○

NAME							
RELATION							
ADDRESS					ZIP CODE		
BOUGHT CARD		○	SENT THE CARD	○	RECEIVED CARD		○

NAME							
RELATION							
ADDRESS					ZIP CODE		
BOUGHT CARD		○	SENT THE CARD	○	RECEIVED CARD		○

NAME							
RELATION							
ADDRESS					ZIP CODE		
BOUGHT CARD		○	SENT THE CARD	○	RECEIVED CARD		○

NAME							
RELATION							
ADDRESS					ZIP CODE		
BOUGHT CARD		○	SENT THE CARD	○	RECEIVED CARD		○

NAME							
RELATION							
ADDRESS					ZIP CODE		
BOUGHT CARD		○	SENT THE CARD	○	RECEIVED CARD		○

Christmas Cards

NAME					
RELATION					
ADDRESS				ZIP CODE	
BOUGHT CARD	○	SENT THE CARD	○	RECEIVED CARD	○

NAME					
RELATION					
ADDRESS				ZIP CODE	
BOUGHT CARD	○	SENT THE CARD	○	RECEIVED CARD	○

NAME					
RELATION					
ADDRESS				ZIP CODE	
BOUGHT CARD	○	SENT THE CARD	○	RECEIVED CARD	○

NAME					
RELATION					
ADDRESS				ZIP CODE	
BOUGHT CARD	○	SENT THE CARD	○	RECEIVED CARD	○

NAME					
RELATION					
ADDRESS				ZIP CODE	
BOUGHT CARD	○	SENT THE CARD	○	RECEIVED CARD	○

NAME					
RELATION					
ADDRESS				ZIP CODE	
BOUGHT CARD	○	SENT THE CARD	○	RECEIVED CARD	○

NAME					
RELATION					
ADDRESS				ZIP CODE	
BOUGHT CARD	○	SENT THE CARD	○	RECEIVED CARD	○

Christmas Cards

NAME					
RELATION					
ADDRESS				ZIP CODE	
BOUGHT CARD	○	SENT THE CARD	○	RECEIVED CARD	○

NAME					
RELATION					
ADDRESS				ZIP CODE	
BOUGHT CARD	○	SENT THE CARD	○	RECEIVED CARD	○

NAME					
RELATION					
ADDRESS				ZIP CODE	
BOUGHT CARD	○	SENT THE CARD	○	RECEIVED CARD	○

NAME					
RELATION					
ADDRESS				ZIP CODE	
BOUGHT CARD	○	SENT THE CARD	○	RECEIVED CARD	○

NAME					
RELATION					
ADDRESS				ZIP CODE	
BOUGHT CARD	○	SENT THE CARD	○	RECEIVED CARD	○

NAME					
RELATION					
ADDRESS				ZIP CODE	
BOUGHT CARD	○	SENT THE CARD	○	RECEIVED CARD	○

NAME					
RELATION					
ADDRESS				ZIP CODE	
BOUGHT CARD	○	SENT THE CARD	○	RECEIVED CARD	○

Christmas Cards

NAME						
RELATION						
ADDRESS				ZIP CODE		
BOUGHT CARD	○	SENT THE CARD	○	RECEIVED CARD	○

NAME						
RELATION						
ADDRESS				ZIP CODE		
BOUGHT CARD	○	SENT THE CARD	○	RECEIVED CARD	○

NAME						
RELATION						
ADDRESS				ZIP CODE		
BOUGHT CARD	○	SENT THE CARD	○	RECEIVED CARD	○

NAME						
RELATION						
ADDRESS				ZIP CODE		
BOUGHT CARD	○	SENT THE CARD	○	RECEIVED CARD	○

NAME						
RELATION						
ADDRESS				ZIP CODE		
BOUGHT CARD	○	SENT THE CARD	○	RECEIVED CARD	○

NAME						
RELATION						
ADDRESS				ZIP CODE		
BOUGHT CARD	○	SENT THE CARD	○	RECEIVED CARD	○

NAME						
RELATION						
ADDRESS				ZIP CODE		
BOUGHT CARD	○	SENT THE CARD	○	RECEIVED CARD	○

Christmas Cards

NAME						
RELATION						
ADDRESS				ZIP CODE		
BOUGHT CARD	○	SENT THE CARD	○	RECEIVED CARD		○

NAME						
RELATION						
ADDRESS				ZIP CODE		
BOUGHT CARD	○	SENT THE CARD	○	RECEIVED CARD		○

NAME						
RELATION						
ADDRESS				ZIP CODE		
BOUGHT CARD	○	SENT THE CARD	○	RECEIVED CARD		○

NAME						
RELATION						
ADDRESS				ZIP CODE		
BOUGHT CARD	○	SENT THE CARD	○	RECEIVED CARD		○

NAME						
RELATION						
ADDRESS				ZIP CODE		
BOUGHT CARD	○	SENT THE CARD	○	RECEIVED CARD		○

NAME						
RELATION						
ADDRESS				ZIP CODE		
BOUGHT CARD	○	SENT THE CARD	○	RECEIVED CARD		○

NAME						
RELATION						
ADDRESS				ZIP CODE		
BOUGHT CARD	○	SENT THE CARD	○	RECEIVED CARD		○

Christmas Cards

NAME						
RELATION						
ADDRESS				ZIP CODE		
BOUGHT CARD	○	SENT THE CARD	○	RECEIVED CARD		○

NAME						
RELATION						
ADDRESS				ZIP CODE		
BOUGHT CARD	○	SENT THE CARD	○	RECEIVED CARD		○

NAME						
RELATION						
ADDRESS				ZIP CODE		
BOUGHT CARD	○	SENT THE CARD	○	RECEIVED CARD		○

NAME						
RELATION						
ADDRESS				ZIP CODE		
BOUGHT CARD	○	SENT THE CARD	○	RECEIVED CARD		○

NAME						
RELATION						
ADDRESS				ZIP CODE		
BOUGHT CARD	○	SENT THE CARD	○	RECEIVED CARD		○

NAME						
RELATION						
ADDRESS				ZIP CODE		
BOUGHT CARD	○	SENT THE CARD	○	RECEIVED CARD		○

NAME						
RELATION						
ADDRESS				ZIP CODE		
BOUGHT CARD	○	SENT THE CARD	○	RECEIVED CARD		○

Christmas Cards

NAME					
RELATION					
ADDRESS			ZIP CODE		
BOUGHT CARD	○	SENT THE CARD	○	RECEIVED CARD	○

NAME					
RELATION					
ADDRESS			ZIP CODE		
BOUGHT CARD	○	SENT THE CARD	○	RECEIVED CARD	○

NAME					
RELATION					
ADDRESS			ZIP CODE		
BOUGHT CARD	○	SENT THE CARD	○	RECEIVED CARD	○

NAME					
RELATION					
ADDRESS			ZIP CODE		
BOUGHT CARD	○	SENT THE CARD	○	RECEIVED CARD	○

NAME					
RELATION					
ADDRESS			ZIP CODE		
BOUGHT CARD	○	SENT THE CARD	○	RECEIVED CARD	○

NAME					
RELATION					
ADDRESS			ZIP CODE		
BOUGHT CARD	○	SENT THE CARD	○	RECEIVED CARD	○

NAME					
RELATION					
ADDRESS			ZIP CODE		
BOUGHT CARD	○	SENT THE CARD	○	RECEIVED CARD	○

Christmas Cards

NAME					
RELATION					
ADDRESS			ZIP CODE		
BOUGHT CARD	○	SENT THE CARD	○	RECEIVED CARD	○

NAME					
RELATION					
ADDRESS			ZIP CODE		
BOUGHT CARD	○	SENT THE CARD	○	RECEIVED CARD	○

NAME					
RELATION					
ADDRESS			ZIP CODE		
BOUGHT CARD	○	SENT THE CARD	○	RECEIVED CARD	○

NAME					
RELATION					
ADDRESS			ZIP CODE		
BOUGHT CARD	○	SENT THE CARD	○	RECEIVED CARD	○

NAME					
RELATION					
ADDRESS			ZIP CODE		
BOUGHT CARD	○	SENT THE CARD	○	RECEIVED CARD	○

NAME					
RELATION					
ADDRESS			ZIP CODE		
BOUGHT CARD	○	SENT THE CARD	○	RECEIVED CARD	○

NAME					
RELATION					
ADDRESS			ZIP CODE		
BOUGHT CARD	○	SENT THE CARD	○	RECEIVED CARD	○

Christmas Cards

NAME						
RELATION						
ADDRESS				ZIP CODE		
BOUGHT CARD	○	SENT THE CARD	○	RECEIVED CARD	○

NAME						
RELATION						
ADDRESS				ZIP CODE		
BOUGHT CARD	○	SENT THE CARD	○	RECEIVED CARD	○

NAME						
RELATION						
ADDRESS				ZIP CODE		
BOUGHT CARD	○	SENT THE CARD	○	RECEIVED CARD	○

NAME						
RELATION						
ADDRESS				ZIP CODE		
BOUGHT CARD	○	SENT THE CARD	○	RECEIVED CARD	○

NAME						
RELATION						
ADDRESS				ZIP CODE		
BOUGHT CARD	○	SENT THE CARD	○	RECEIVED CARD	○

NAME						
RELATION						
ADDRESS				ZIP CODE		
BOUGHT CARD	○	SENT THE CARD	○	RECEIVED CARD	○

NAME						
RELATION						
ADDRESS				ZIP CODE		
BOUGHT CARD	○	SENT THE CARD	○	RECEIVED CARD	○

Christmas Cards

NAME					
RELATION					
ADDRESS			ZIP CODE		
BOUGHT CARD	○	SENT THE CARD	○	RECEIVED CARD	○

NAME					
RELATION					
ADDRESS			ZIP CODE		
BOUGHT CARD	○	SENT THE CARD	○	RECEIVED CARD	○

NAME					
RELATION					
ADDRESS			ZIP CODE		
BOUGHT CARD	○	SENT THE CARD	○	RECEIVED CARD	○

NAME					
RELATION					
ADDRESS			ZIP CODE		
BOUGHT CARD	○	SENT THE CARD	○	RECEIVED CARD	○

NAME					
RELATION					
ADDRESS			ZIP CODE		
BOUGHT CARD	○	SENT THE CARD	○	RECEIVED CARD	○

NAME					
RELATION					
ADDRESS			ZIP CODE		
BOUGHT CARD	○	SENT THE CARD	○	RECEIVED CARD	○

NAME					
RELATION					
ADDRESS			ZIP CODE		
BOUGHT CARD	○	SENT THE CARD	○	RECEIVED CARD	○

Christmas Cards

NAME					
RELATION					
ADDRESS			ZIP CODE		
BOUGHT CARD	○	SENT THE CARD	○	RECEIVED CARD	○

NAME					
RELATION					
ADDRESS			ZIP CODE		
BOUGHT CARD	○	SENT THE CARD	○	RECEIVED CARD	○

NAME					
RELATION					
ADDRESS			ZIP CODE		
BOUGHT CARD	○	SENT THE CARD	○	RECEIVED CARD	○

NAME					
RELATION					
ADDRESS			ZIP CODE		
BOUGHT CARD	○	SENT THE CARD	○	RECEIVED CARD	○

NAME					
RELATION					
ADDRESS			ZIP CODE		
BOUGHT CARD	○	SENT THE CARD	○	RECEIVED CARD	○

NAME					
RELATION					
ADDRESS			ZIP CODE		
BOUGHT CARD	○	SENT THE CARD	○	RECEIVED CARD	○

NAME					
RELATION					
ADDRESS			ZIP CODE		
BOUGHT CARD	○	SENT THE CARD	○	RECEIVED CARD	○

Christmas Cards

NAME					
RELATION					
ADDRESS			ZIP CODE		
BOUGHT CARD	○	SENT THE CARD	○	RECEIVED CARD	○

NAME					
RELATION					
ADDRESS			ZIP CODE		
BOUGHT CARD	○	SENT THE CARD	○	RECEIVED CARD	○

NAME					
RELATION					
ADDRESS			ZIP CODE		
BOUGHT CARD	○	SENT THE CARD	○	RECEIVED CARD	○

NAME					
RELATION					
ADDRESS			ZIP CODE		
BOUGHT CARD	○	SENT THE CARD	○	RECEIVED CARD	○

NAME					
RELATION					
ADDRESS			ZIP CODE		
BOUGHT CARD	○	SENT THE CARD	○	RECEIVED CARD	○

NAME					
RELATION					
ADDRESS			ZIP CODE		
BOUGHT CARD	○	SENT THE CARD	○	RECEIVED CARD	○

NAME					
RELATION					
ADDRESS			ZIP CODE		
BOUGHT CARD	○	SENT THE CARD	○	RECEIVED CARD	○

Christmas Cards

NAME					
RELATION					
ADDRESS			ZIP CODE		
BOUGHT CARD	○	SENT THE CARD	○	RECEIVED CARD	○

NAME					
RELATION					
ADDRESS			ZIP CODE		
BOUGHT CARD	○	SENT THE CARD	○	RECEIVED CARD	○

NAME					
RELATION					
ADDRESS			ZIP CODE		
BOUGHT CARD	○	SENT THE CARD	○	RECEIVED CARD	○

NAME					
RELATION					
ADDRESS			ZIP CODE		
BOUGHT CARD	○	SENT THE CARD	○	RECEIVED CARD	○

NAME					
RELATION					
ADDRESS			ZIP CODE		
BOUGHT CARD	○	SENT THE CARD	○	RECEIVED CARD	○

NAME					
RELATION					
ADDRESS			ZIP CODE		
BOUGHT CARD	○	SENT THE CARD	○	RECEIVED CARD	○

NAME					
RELATION					
ADDRESS			ZIP CODE		
BOUGHT CARD	○	SENT THE CARD	○	RECEIVED CARD	○

Christmas Cards

NAME					
RELATION					
ADDRESS			ZIP CODE		
BOUGHT CARD	○	SENT THE CARD	○	RECEIVED CARD	○

NAME					
RELATION					
ADDRESS			ZIP CODE		
BOUGHT CARD	○	SENT THE CARD	○	RECEIVED CARD	○

NAME					
RELATION					
ADDRESS			ZIP CODE		
BOUGHT CARD	○	SENT THE CARD	○	RECEIVED CARD	○

NAME					
RELATION					
ADDRESS			ZIP CODE		
BOUGHT CARD	○	SENT THE CARD	○	RECEIVED CARD	○

NAME					
RELATION					
ADDRESS			ZIP CODE		
BOUGHT CARD	○	SENT THE CARD	○	RECEIVED CARD	○

NAME					
RELATION					
ADDRESS			ZIP CODE		
BOUGHT CARD	○	SENT THE CARD	○	RECEIVED CARD	○

NAME					
RELATION					
ADDRESS			ZIP CODE		
BOUGHT CARD	○	SENT THE CARD	○	RECEIVED CARD	○

Christmas Cards

NAME	
RELATION	
ADDRESS	ZIP CODE
BOUGHT CARD ○	SENT THE CARD ○	RECEIVED CARD ○

NAME	
RELATION	
ADDRESS	ZIP CODE
BOUGHT CARD ○	SENT THE CARD ○	RECEIVED CARD ○

NAME	
RELATION	
ADDRESS	ZIP CODE
BOUGHT CARD ○	SENT THE CARD ○	RECEIVED CARD ○

NAME	
RELATION	
ADDRESS	ZIP CODE
BOUGHT CARD ○	SENT THE CARD ○	RECEIVED CARD ○

NAME	
RELATION	
ADDRESS	ZIP CODE
BOUGHT CARD ○	SENT THE CARD ○	RECEIVED CARD ○

NAME	
RELATION	
ADDRESS	ZIP CODE
BOUGHT CARD ○	SENT THE CARD ○	RECEIVED CARD ○

NAME	
RELATION	
ADDRESS	ZIP CODE
BOUGHT CARD ○	SENT THE CARD ○	RECEIVED CARD ○

Christmas Cards

NAME					
RELATION					
ADDRESS			ZIP CODE		
BOUGHT CARD	○	SENT THE CARD	○	RECEIVED CARD	○

NAME					
RELATION					
ADDRESS			ZIP CODE		
BOUGHT CARD	○	SENT THE CARD	○	RECEIVED CARD	○

NAME					
RELATION					
ADDRESS			ZIP CODE		
BOUGHT CARD	○	SENT THE CARD	○	RECEIVED CARD	○

NAME					
RELATION					
ADDRESS			ZIP CODE		
BOUGHT CARD	○	SENT THE CARD	○	RECEIVED CARD	○

NAME					
RELATION					
ADDRESS			ZIP CODE		
BOUGHT CARD	○	SENT THE CARD	○	RECEIVED CARD	○

NAME					
RELATION					
ADDRESS			ZIP CODE		
BOUGHT CARD	○	SENT THE CARD	○	RECEIVED CARD	○

NAME					
RELATION					
ADDRESS			ZIP CODE		
BOUGHT CARD	○	SENT THE CARD	○	RECEIVED CARD	○

Christmas Cards

NAME							
RELATION							
ADDRESS					ZIP CODE		
BOUGHT CARD		○	SENT THE CARD	○	RECEIVED CARD		○

NAME							
RELATION							
ADDRESS					ZIP CODE		
BOUGHT CARD		○	SENT THE CARD	○	RECEIVED CARD		○

NAME							
RELATION							
ADDRESS					ZIP CODE		
BOUGHT CARD		○	SENT THE CARD	○	RECEIVED CARD		○

NAME							
RELATION							
ADDRESS					ZIP CODE		
BOUGHT CARD		○	SENT THE CARD	○	RECEIVED CARD		○

NAME							
RELATION							
ADDRESS					ZIP CODE		
BOUGHT CARD		○	SENT THE CARD	○	RECEIVED CARD		○

NAME							
RELATION							
ADDRESS					ZIP CODE		
BOUGHT CARD		○	SENT THE CARD	○	RECEIVED CARD		○

NAME							
RELATION							
ADDRESS					ZIP CODE		
BOUGHT CARD		○	SENT THE CARD	○	RECEIVED CARD		○

Christmas Cards

NAME					
RELATION					
ADDRESS			ZIP CODE		
BOUGHT CARD	○	SENT THE CARD	○	RECEIVED CARD	○

NAME					
RELATION					
ADDRESS			ZIP CODE		
BOUGHT CARD	○	SENT THE CARD	○	RECEIVED CARD	○

NAME					
RELATION					
ADDRESS			ZIP CODE		
BOUGHT CARD	○	SENT THE CARD	○	RECEIVED CARD	○

NAME					
RELATION					
ADDRESS			ZIP CODE		
BOUGHT CARD	○	SENT THE CARD	○	RECEIVED CARD	○

NAME					
RELATION					
ADDRESS			ZIP CODE		
BOUGHT CARD	○	SENT THE CARD	○	RECEIVED CARD	○

NAME					
RELATION					
ADDRESS			ZIP CODE		
BOUGHT CARD	○	SENT THE CARD	○	RECEIVED CARD	○

NAME					
RELATION					
ADDRESS			ZIP CODE		
BOUGHT CARD	○	SENT THE CARD	○	RECEIVED CARD	○

Christmas Cards

NAME					
RELATION					
ADDRESS			ZIP CODE		
BOUGHT CARD	○	SENT THE CARD	○	RECEIVED CARD	○

NAME					
RELATION					
ADDRESS			ZIP CODE		
BOUGHT CARD	○	SENT THE CARD	○	RECEIVED CARD	○

NAME					
RELATION					
ADDRESS			ZIP CODE		
BOUGHT CARD	○	SENT THE CARD	○	RECEIVED CARD	○

NAME					
RELATION					
ADDRESS			ZIP CODE		
BOUGHT CARD	○	SENT THE CARD	○	RECEIVED CARD	○

NAME					
RELATION					
ADDRESS			ZIP CODE		
BOUGHT CARD	○	SENT THE CARD	○	RECEIVED CARD	○

NAME					
RELATION					
ADDRESS			ZIP CODE		
BOUGHT CARD	○	SENT THE CARD	○	RECEIVED CARD	○

NAME					
RELATION					
ADDRESS			ZIP CODE		
BOUGHT CARD	○	SENT THE CARD	○	RECEIVED CARD	○

Christmas Cards

NAME					
RELATION					
ADDRESS			ZIP CODE		
BOUGHT CARD	○	SENT THE CARD	○	RECEIVED CARD	○

NAME					
RELATION					
ADDRESS			ZIP CODE		
BOUGHT CARD	○	SENT THE CARD	○	RECEIVED CARD	○

NAME					
RELATION					
ADDRESS			ZIP CODE		
BOUGHT CARD	○	SENT THE CARD	○	RECEIVED CARD	○

NAME					
RELATION					
ADDRESS			ZIP CODE		
BOUGHT CARD	○	SENT THE CARD	○	RECEIVED CARD	○

NAME					
RELATION					
ADDRESS			ZIP CODE		
BOUGHT CARD	○	SENT THE CARD	○	RECEIVED CARD	○

NAME					
RELATION					
ADDRESS			ZIP CODE		
BOUGHT CARD	○	SENT THE CARD	○	RECEIVED CARD	○

NAME					
RELATION					
ADDRESS			ZIP CODE		
BOUGHT CARD	○	SENT THE CARD	○	RECEIVED CARD	○

Christmas Cards

NAME					
RELATION					
ADDRESS				ZIP CODE	
BOUGHT CARD	○	SENT THE CARD	○	RECEIVED CARD	○

NAME					
RELATION					
ADDRESS				ZIP CODE	
BOUGHT CARD	○	SENT THE CARD	○	RECEIVED CARD	○

NAME					
RELATION					
ADDRESS				ZIP CODE	
BOUGHT CARD	○	SENT THE CARD	○	RECEIVED CARD	○

NAME					
RELATION					
ADDRESS				ZIP CODE	
BOUGHT CARD	○	SENT THE CARD	○	RECEIVED CARD	○

NAME					
RELATION					
ADDRESS				ZIP CODE	
BOUGHT CARD	○	SENT THE CARD	○	RECEIVED CARD	○

NAME					
RELATION					
ADDRESS				ZIP CODE	
BOUGHT CARD	○	SENT THE CARD	○	RECEIVED CARD	○

NAME					
RELATION					
ADDRESS				ZIP CODE	
BOUGHT CARD	○	SENT THE CARD	○	RECEIVED CARD	○

Christmas Cards

NAME					
RELATION					
ADDRESS			ZIP CODE		
BOUGHT CARD	○	SENT THE CARD	○	RECEIVED CARD	○

NAME					
RELATION					
ADDRESS			ZIP CODE		
BOUGHT CARD	○	SENT THE CARD	○	RECEIVED CARD	○

NAME					
RELATION					
ADDRESS			ZIP CODE		
BOUGHT CARD	○	SENT THE CARD	○	RECEIVED CARD	○

NAME					
RELATION					
ADDRESS			ZIP CODE		
BOUGHT CARD	○	SENT THE CARD	○	RECEIVED CARD	○

NAME					
RELATION					
ADDRESS			ZIP CODE		
BOUGHT CARD	○	SENT THE CARD	○	RECEIVED CARD	○

NAME					
RELATION					
ADDRESS			ZIP CODE		
BOUGHT CARD	○	SENT THE CARD	○	RECEIVED CARD	○

NAME					
RELATION					
ADDRESS			ZIP CODE		
BOUGHT CARD	○	SENT THE CARD	○	RECEIVED CARD	○

Christmas Cards

NAME							
RELATION							
ADDRESS				ZIP CODE			
BOUGHT CARD		○	SENT THE CARD	○	RECEIVED CARD		○

NAME							
RELATION							
ADDRESS				ZIP CODE			
BOUGHT CARD		○	SENT THE CARD	○	RECEIVED CARD		○

NAME							
RELATION							
ADDRESS				ZIP CODE			
BOUGHT CARD		○	SENT THE CARD	○	RECEIVED CARD		○

NAME							
RELATION							
ADDRESS				ZIP CODE			
BOUGHT CARD		○	SENT THE CARD	○	RECEIVED CARD		○

NAME							
RELATION							
ADDRESS				ZIP CODE			
BOUGHT CARD		○	SENT THE CARD	○	RECEIVED CARD		○

NAME							
RELATION							
ADDRESS				ZIP CODE			
BOUGHT CARD		○	SENT THE CARD	○	RECEIVED CARD		○

NAME							
RELATION							
ADDRESS				ZIP CODE			
BOUGHT CARD		○	SENT THE CARD	○	RECEIVED CARD		○

Christmas Cards

NAME					
RELATION					
ADDRESS			ZIP CODE		
BOUGHT CARD	○	SENT THE CARD	○	RECEIVED CARD	○

NAME					
RELATION					
ADDRESS			ZIP CODE		
BOUGHT CARD	○	SENT THE CARD	○	RECEIVED CARD	○

NAME					
RELATION					
ADDRESS			ZIP CODE		
BOUGHT CARD	○	SENT THE CARD	○	RECEIVED CARD	○

NAME					
RELATION					
ADDRESS			ZIP CODE		
BOUGHT CARD	○	SENT THE CARD	○	RECEIVED CARD	○

NAME					
RELATION					
ADDRESS			ZIP CODE		
BOUGHT CARD	○	SENT THE CARD	○	RECEIVED CARD	○

NAME					
RELATION					
ADDRESS			ZIP CODE		
BOUGHT CARD	○	SENT THE CARD	○	RECEIVED CARD	○

NAME					
RELATION					
ADDRESS			ZIP CODE		
BOUGHT CARD	○	SENT THE CARD	○	RECEIVED CARD	○

Christmas Cards

NAME					
RELATION					
ADDRESS				ZIP CODE	
BOUGHT CARD	○	SENT THE CARD	○	RECEIVED CARD	○

NAME					
RELATION					
ADDRESS				ZIP CODE	
BOUGHT CARD	○	SENT THE CARD	○	RECEIVED CARD	○

NAME					
RELATION					
ADDRESS				ZIP CODE	
BOUGHT CARD	○	SENT THE CARD	○	RECEIVED CARD	○

NAME					
RELATION					
ADDRESS				ZIP CODE	
BOUGHT CARD	○	SENT THE CARD	○	RECEIVED CARD	○

NAME					
RELATION					
ADDRESS				ZIP CODE	
BOUGHT CARD	○	SENT THE CARD	○	RECEIVED CARD	○

NAME					
RELATION					
ADDRESS				ZIP CODE	
BOUGHT CARD	○	SENT THE CARD	○	RECEIVED CARD	○

NAME					
RELATION					
ADDRESS				ZIP CODE	
BOUGHT CARD	○	SENT THE CARD	○	RECEIVED CARD	○

Christmas Cards

NAME					
RELATION					
ADDRESS				ZIP CODE	
BOUGHT CARD	○	SENT THE CARD	○	RECEIVED CARD	○

NAME					
RELATION					
ADDRESS				ZIP CODE	
BOUGHT CARD	○	SENT THE CARD	○	RECEIVED CARD	○

NAME					
RELATION					
ADDRESS				ZIP CODE	
BOUGHT CARD	○	SENT THE CARD	○	RECEIVED CARD	○

NAME					
RELATION					
ADDRESS				ZIP CODE	
BOUGHT CARD	○	SENT THE CARD	○	RECEIVED CARD	○

NAME					
RELATION					
ADDRESS				ZIP CODE	
BOUGHT CARD	○	SENT THE CARD	○	RECEIVED CARD	○

NAME					
RELATION					
ADDRESS				ZIP CODE	
BOUGHT CARD	○	SENT THE CARD	○	RECEIVED CARD	○

NAME					
RELATION					
ADDRESS				ZIP CODE	
BOUGHT CARD	○	SENT THE CARD	○	RECEIVED CARD	○

Christmas Cards

NAME							
RELATION							
ADDRESS					ZIP CODE		
BOUGHT CARD		○	SENT THE CARD	○	RECEIVED CARD		○

NAME							
RELATION							
ADDRESS					ZIP CODE		
BOUGHT CARD		○	SENT THE CARD	○	RECEIVED CARD		○

NAME							
RELATION							
ADDRESS					ZIP CODE		
BOUGHT CARD		○	SENT THE CARD	○	RECEIVED CARD		○

NAME							
RELATION							
ADDRESS					ZIP CODE		
BOUGHT CARD		○	SENT THE CARD	○	RECEIVED CARD		○

NAME							
RELATION							
ADDRESS					ZIP CODE		
BOUGHT CARD		○	SENT THE CARD	○	RECEIVED CARD		○

NAME							
RELATION							
ADDRESS					ZIP CODE		
BOUGHT CARD		○	SENT THE CARD	○	RECEIVED CARD		○

NAME							
RELATION							
ADDRESS					ZIP CODE		
BOUGHT CARD		○	SENT THE CARD	○	RECEIVED CARD		○

Christmas Cards

NAME					
RELATION					
ADDRESS			ZIP CODE		
BOUGHT CARD	○	SENT THE CARD	○	RECEIVED CARD	○

NAME					
RELATION					
ADDRESS			ZIP CODE		
BOUGHT CARD	○	SENT THE CARD	○	RECEIVED CARD	○

NAME					
RELATION					
ADDRESS			ZIP CODE		
BOUGHT CARD	○	SENT THE CARD	○	RECEIVED CARD	○

NAME					
RELATION					
ADDRESS			ZIP CODE		
BOUGHT CARD	○	SENT THE CARD	○	RECEIVED CARD	○

NAME					
RELATION					
ADDRESS			ZIP CODE		
BOUGHT CARD	○	SENT THE CARD	○	RECEIVED CARD	○

NAME					
RELATION					
ADDRESS			ZIP CODE		
BOUGHT CARD	○	SENT THE CARD	○	RECEIVED CARD	○

NAME					
RELATION					
ADDRESS			ZIP CODE		
BOUGHT CARD	○	SENT THE CARD	○	RECEIVED CARD	○

Christmas Cards

NAME						
RELATION						
ADDRESS				ZIP CODE		
BOUGHT CARD	○	SENT THE CARD	○	RECEIVED CARD		○

NAME						
RELATION						
ADDRESS				ZIP CODE		
BOUGHT CARD	○	SENT THE CARD	○	RECEIVED CARD		○

NAME						
RELATION						
ADDRESS				ZIP CODE		
BOUGHT CARD	○	SENT THE CARD	○	RECEIVED CARD		○

NAME						
RELATION						
ADDRESS				ZIP CODE		
BOUGHT CARD	○	SENT THE CARD	○	RECEIVED CARD		○

NAME						
RELATION						
ADDRESS				ZIP CODE		
BOUGHT CARD	○	SENT THE CARD	○	RECEIVED CARD		○

NAME						
RELATION						
ADDRESS				ZIP CODE		
BOUGHT CARD	○	SENT THE CARD	○	RECEIVED CARD		○

NAME						
RELATION						
ADDRESS				ZIP CODE		
BOUGHT CARD	○	SENT THE CARD	○	RECEIVED CARD		○

Christmas Cards

NAME					
RELATION					
ADDRESS			ZIP CODE		
BOUGHT CARD	○	SENT THE CARD	○	RECEIVED CARD	○

NAME					
RELATION					
ADDRESS			ZIP CODE		
BOUGHT CARD	○	SENT THE CARD	○	RECEIVED CARD	○

NAME					
RELATION					
ADDRESS			ZIP CODE		
BOUGHT CARD	○	SENT THE CARD	○	RECEIVED CARD	○

NAME					
RELATION					
ADDRESS			ZIP CODE		
BOUGHT CARD	○	SENT THE CARD	○	RECEIVED CARD	○

NAME					
RELATION					
ADDRESS			ZIP CODE		
BOUGHT CARD	○	SENT THE CARD	○	RECEIVED CARD	○

NAME					
RELATION					
ADDRESS			ZIP CODE		
BOUGHT CARD	○	SENT THE CARD	○	RECEIVED CARD	○

NAME					
RELATION					
ADDRESS			ZIP CODE		
BOUGHT CARD	○	SENT THE CARD	○	RECEIVED CARD	○

Christmas Cards

NAME					
RELATION					
ADDRESS			ZIP CODE		
BOUGHT CARD	○	SENT THE CARD	○	RECEIVED CARD	○

NAME					
RELATION					
ADDRESS			ZIP CODE		
BOUGHT CARD	○	SENT THE CARD	○	RECEIVED CARD	○

NAME					
RELATION					
ADDRESS			ZIP CODE		
BOUGHT CARD	○	SENT THE CARD	○	RECEIVED CARD	○

NAME					
RELATION					
ADDRESS			ZIP CODE		
BOUGHT CARD	○	SENT THE CARD	○	RECEIVED CARD	○

NAME					
RELATION					
ADDRESS			ZIP CODE		
BOUGHT CARD	○	SENT THE CARD	○	RECEIVED CARD	○

NAME					
RELATION					
ADDRESS			ZIP CODE		
BOUGHT CARD	○	SENT THE CARD	○	RECEIVED CARD	○

NAME					
RELATION					
ADDRESS			ZIP CODE		
BOUGHT CARD	○	SENT THE CARD	○	RECEIVED CARD	○

Christmas Cards

NAME					
RELATION					
ADDRESS			ZIP CODE		
BOUGHT CARD	○	SENT THE CARD	○	RECEIVED CARD	○

NAME					
RELATION					
ADDRESS			ZIP CODE		
BOUGHT CARD	○	SENT THE CARD	○	RECEIVED CARD	○

NAME					
RELATION					
ADDRESS			ZIP CODE		
BOUGHT CARD	○	SENT THE CARD	○	RECEIVED CARD	○

NAME					
RELATION					
ADDRESS			ZIP CODE		
BOUGHT CARD	○	SENT THE CARD	○	RECEIVED CARD	○

NAME					
RELATION					
ADDRESS			ZIP CODE		
BOUGHT CARD	○	SENT THE CARD	○	RECEIVED CARD	○

NAME					
RELATION					
ADDRESS			ZIP CODE		
BOUGHT CARD	○	SENT THE CARD	○	RECEIVED CARD	○

NAME					
RELATION					
ADDRESS			ZIP CODE		
BOUGHT CARD	○	SENT THE CARD	○	RECEIVED CARD	○

Christmas Cards

NAME					
RELATION					
ADDRESS				ZIP CODE	
BOUGHT CARD	○	SENT THE CARD	○	RECEIVED CARD	○

NAME					
RELATION					
ADDRESS				ZIP CODE	
BOUGHT CARD	○	SENT THE CARD	○	RECEIVED CARD	○

NAME					
RELATION					
ADDRESS				ZIP CODE	
BOUGHT CARD	○	SENT THE CARD	○	RECEIVED CARD	○

NAME					
RELATION					
ADDRESS				ZIP CODE	
BOUGHT CARD	○	SENT THE CARD	○	RECEIVED CARD	○

NAME					
RELATION					
ADDRESS				ZIP CODE	
BOUGHT CARD	○	SENT THE CARD	○	RECEIVED CARD	○

NAME					
RELATION					
ADDRESS				ZIP CODE	
BOUGHT CARD	○	SENT THE CARD	○	RECEIVED CARD	○

NAME					
RELATION					
ADDRESS				ZIP CODE	
BOUGHT CARD	○	SENT THE CARD	○	RECEIVED CARD	○

Christmas Cards

NAME					
RELATION					
ADDRESS			ZIP CODE		
BOUGHT CARD	○	SENT THE CARD	○	RECEIVED CARD	○

NAME					
RELATION					
ADDRESS			ZIP CODE		
BOUGHT CARD	○	SENT THE CARD	○	RECEIVED CARD	○

NAME					
RELATION					
ADDRESS			ZIP CODE		
BOUGHT CARD	○	SENT THE CARD	○	RECEIVED CARD	○

NAME					
RELATION					
ADDRESS			ZIP CODE		
BOUGHT CARD	○	SENT THE CARD	○	RECEIVED CARD	○

NAME					
RELATION					
ADDRESS			ZIP CODE		
BOUGHT CARD	○	SENT THE CARD	○	RECEIVED CARD	○

NAME					
RELATION					
ADDRESS			ZIP CODE		
BOUGHT CARD	○	SENT THE CARD	○	RECEIVED CARD	○

NAME					
RELATION					
ADDRESS			ZIP CODE		
BOUGHT CARD	○	SENT THE CARD	○	RECEIVED CARD	○

Christmas Cards

NAME						
RELATION						
ADDRESS				ZIP CODE		
BOUGHT CARD	○	SENT THE CARD	○	RECEIVED CARD		○

NAME						
RELATION						
ADDRESS				ZIP CODE		
BOUGHT CARD	○	SENT THE CARD	○	RECEIVED CARD		○

NAME						
RELATION						
ADDRESS				ZIP CODE		
BOUGHT CARD	○	SENT THE CARD	○	RECEIVED CARD		○

NAME						
RELATION						
ADDRESS				ZIP CODE		
BOUGHT CARD	○	SENT THE CARD	○	RECEIVED CARD		○

NAME						
RELATION						
ADDRESS				ZIP CODE		
BOUGHT CARD	○	SENT THE CARD	○	RECEIVED CARD		○

NAME						
RELATION						
ADDRESS				ZIP CODE		
BOUGHT CARD	○	SENT THE CARD	○	RECEIVED CARD		○

NAME						
RELATION						
ADDRESS				ZIP CODE		
BOUGHT CARD	○	SENT THE CARD	○	RECEIVED CARD		○

Christmas Cards

NAME					
RELATION					
ADDRESS			ZIP CODE		
BOUGHT CARD	○	SENT THE CARD	○	RECEIVED CARD	○

NAME					
RELATION					
ADDRESS			ZIP CODE		
BOUGHT CARD	○	SENT THE CARD	○	RECEIVED CARD	○

NAME					
RELATION					
ADDRESS			ZIP CODE		
BOUGHT CARD	○	SENT THE CARD	○	RECEIVED CARD	○

NAME					
RELATION					
ADDRESS			ZIP CODE		
BOUGHT CARD	○	SENT THE CARD	○	RECEIVED CARD	○

NAME					
RELATION					
ADDRESS			ZIP CODE		
BOUGHT CARD	○	SENT THE CARD	○	RECEIVED CARD	○

NAME					
RELATION					
ADDRESS			ZIP CODE		
BOUGHT CARD	○	SENT THE CARD	○	RECEIVED CARD	○

NAME					
RELATION					
ADDRESS			ZIP CODE		
BOUGHT CARD	○	SENT THE CARD	○	RECEIVED CARD	○

Christmas Cards

NAME							
RELATION							
ADDRESS					ZIP CODE		
BOUGHT CARD		○	SENT THE CARD	○	RECEIVED CARD		○

NAME							
RELATION							
ADDRESS					ZIP CODE		
BOUGHT CARD		○	SENT THE CARD	○	RECEIVED CARD		○

NAME							
RELATION							
ADDRESS					ZIP CODE		
BOUGHT CARD		○	SENT THE CARD	○	RECEIVED CARD		○

NAME							
RELATION							
ADDRESS					ZIP CODE		
BOUGHT CARD		○	SENT THE CARD	○	RECEIVED CARD		○

NAME							
RELATION							
ADDRESS					ZIP CODE		
BOUGHT CARD		○	SENT THE CARD	○	RECEIVED CARD		○

NAME							
RELATION							
ADDRESS					ZIP CODE		
BOUGHT CARD		○	SENT THE CARD	○	RECEIVED CARD		○

NAME							
RELATION							
ADDRESS					ZIP CODE		
BOUGHT CARD		○	SENT THE CARD	○	RECEIVED CARD		○

Christmas Cards

NAME					
RELATION					
ADDRESS			ZIP CODE		
BOUGHT CARD	○	SENT THE CARD	○	RECEIVED CARD	○

NAME					
RELATION					
ADDRESS			ZIP CODE		
BOUGHT CARD	○	SENT THE CARD	○	RECEIVED CARD	○

NAME					
RELATION					
ADDRESS			ZIP CODE		
BOUGHT CARD	○	SENT THE CARD	○	RECEIVED CARD	○

NAME					
RELATION					
ADDRESS			ZIP CODE		
BOUGHT CARD	○	SENT THE CARD	○	RECEIVED CARD	○

NAME					
RELATION					
ADDRESS			ZIP CODE		
BOUGHT CARD	○	SENT THE CARD	○	RECEIVED CARD	○

NAME					
RELATION					
ADDRESS			ZIP CODE		
BOUGHT CARD	○	SENT THE CARD	○	RECEIVED CARD	○

NAME					
RELATION					
ADDRESS			ZIP CODE		
BOUGHT CARD	○	SENT THE CARD	○	RECEIVED CARD	○

www.ingramcontent.com/pod-product-compliance
Lightning Source LLC
Chambersburg PA
CBHW071317080526
44587CB00018B/3253